Guess Who
Bites

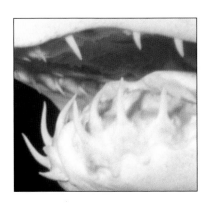

Sharon Gordon

BENCHMARK BOOKS

MARSHALL CAVENDISH
NEW YORK

My home is in the sea.

I am a big fish.

I have a long, smooth body.

It has *scales* on it.

I breathe through slits called *gills*.

My gills take air from the water.

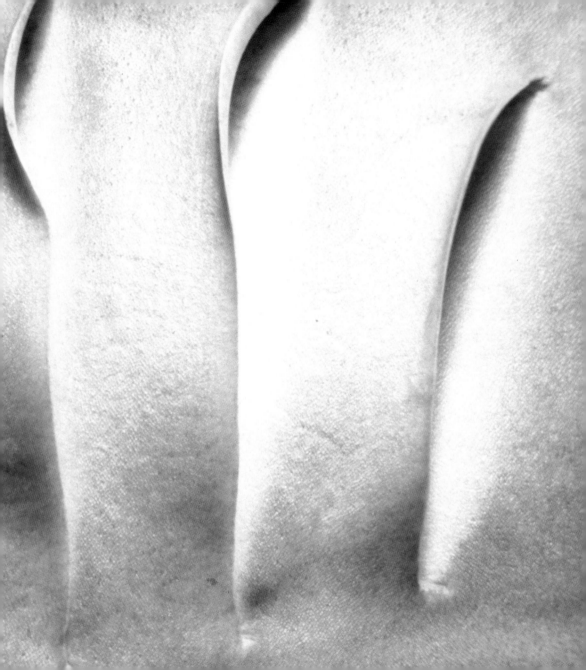

I can swim and dive very fast.

My tail *fin* moves me forward.

My side fins lift and turn me.

The fin on my back stops me from rolling over.

Do you see it above the water?

It is easy for me to find food.

I can smell a fish from far away.

I can see well underwater.

My eyes open wide.

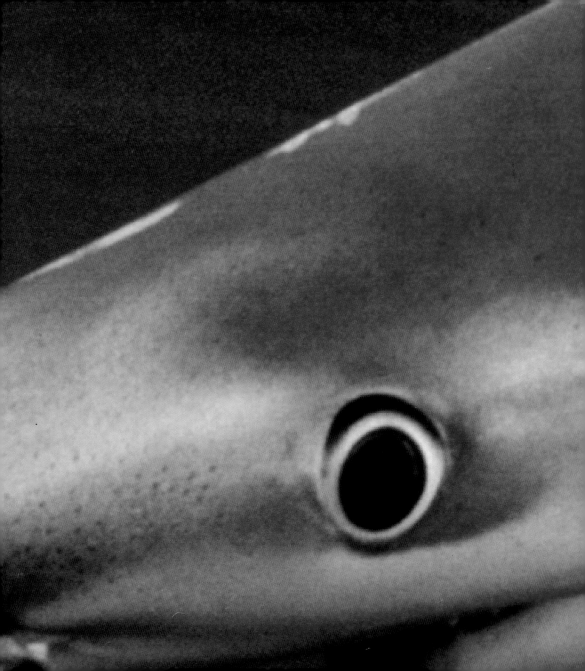

I have special eyelids.

They close in a fight.

They keep my eyes safe.

I have strong jaws.

My bite is powerful.

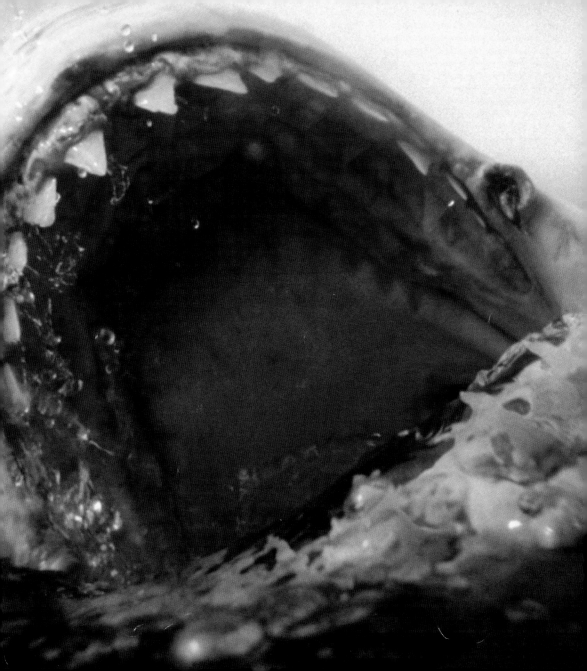

I have rows of big, sharp teeth.

I use them to bite and crush my food.

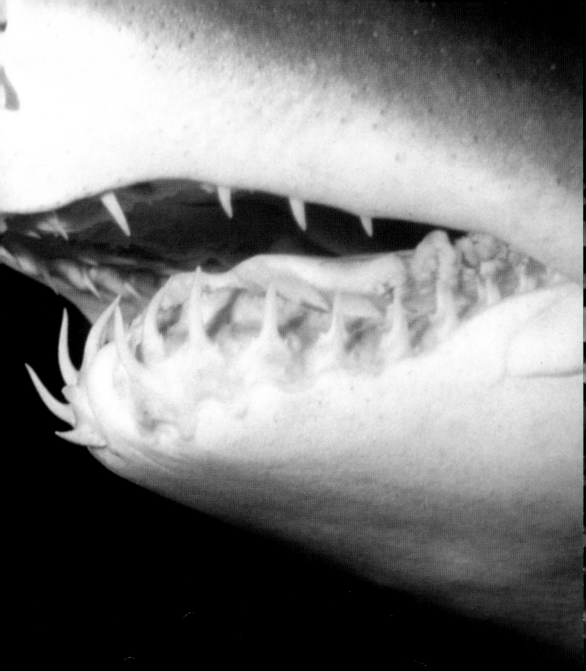

My baby is called a *pup*.

It can swim and bite right away!

I am hungry now.

Time to eat!

Who am I?

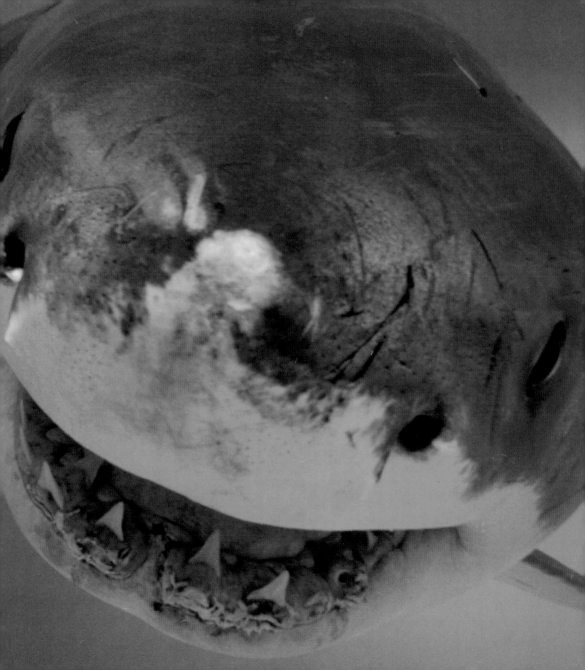

I am a shark!

Who am I?

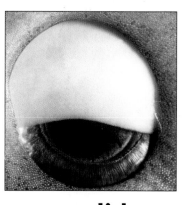

eyelid

fin

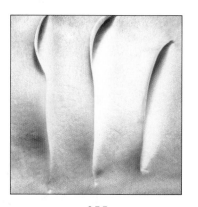

gills

scales

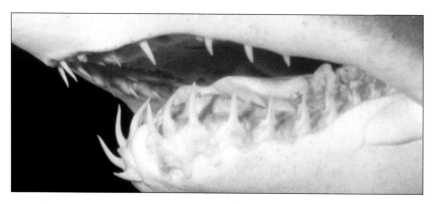

teeth

Challenge Words

fins
The thin, flat parts of a shark that it uses to swim.

gills
The parts of a shark's body that it uses to breathe.

pup
A baby shark.

scales
The small, flat pieces of skin on a shark's body.

29

Index

Page numbers in **boldface** are illustrations.

About the Author

Sharon Gordon has written many books for young children. She has always worked as an editor. Sharon and her husband Bruce have three children, Douglas, Katie, and Laura, and one spoiled pooch, Samantha. They live in Midland Park, New Jersey.

With thanks to Nanci Vargus, Ed.D. and Beth Walker Gambro, reading consultants

Benchmark Books
Marshall Cavendish
99 White Plains Road
Tarrytown, New York 10591-9001
www.marshallcavendish.com

Library of Congress Cataloging-in-Publication Data

Gordon, Sharon.
Guess who bites / by Sharon Gordon.
p. cm. — (Bookworms: Guess Who)
Includes index.
ISBN 0-7614-1766-4
1. Sharks—Juvenile literature. I. Title
II. Series: Gordon, Sharon. Bookworms: Guess Who.

QL638.9.G65 2004
597.3—dc22
2004003410

Photo Research by Anne Burns Images

Cover Photo by *Animals Animals*/Carmela Leszczynski

The photographs in this book are used with the permission and through the courtesy of:
Animals Animals: pp. 1, 21, 29 Carmela Leszczynski; p. 3 Marion Bacon; pp. 5,
28 (bottom r.) Herb Segars; pp. 11, 19, 28 (top r.) James Watt; pp. 13, 15 Bob Cranston;
p. 25 OSF/Fleetham,D. *Peter Arnold*: pp. 7, 17, 28 (top & bottom l.) Jeff Rotman;
pp. 9, 27 Kelvin Aitkin. *Corbis*: p. 23 Jeff Rotman.

Series design by Becky Terhune

Printed in China
1 3 5 6 4 2